THE OFFICE
LITTLE INSTRUCTION
BOOK

THE OFFICE LIFE
LITTLE INSTRUCTION
BOOK

Holly Budd

Thorsons
An Imprint of HarperCollins*Publishers*

Thorsons
An Imprint of HarperCollins*Publishers*
77– 85 Fulham Palace Road,
Hammersmith, London W6 8JB
1160 Battery Street,
San Francisco, California 94111–1213

Published by Thorsons 1996
1 3 5 7 9 10 8 6 4 2

A catalogue record for this book is available from the British Library

ISBN 0 7225 3287 3

Printed in Great Britain by
HarperCollinsManufacturing Glasgow

Introduction

Everyone, not only those who staff them, is profoundly affected by what happens in offices. Major areas of life – health, education, money, housing, food, drink, clothing, what we read, watch and hear – are shaped by decisions made in offices. How people behave there touches us all. 'They' are not different from us; they *are* us, in different roles.

The office is also the stage on which many of life's dramas are enacted. There is success and failure, quiet tragedy, obvious humour, distorting jealousy, blinding ambition, generosity, kindness, truth, deceit, anger, lust and love. The office can be dull, funny, passionate and sad, and all that happens is played out in a variety of codes and conventions of a sophistication and subtlety we take surprisingly for granted.

It is not representative of all life. The old, the young, the sick, the illiterate and the poorest are not there. It may be that offices as we know them will change with changing technology, but so far technological change has always created more jobs as money and goods are traded more. If the office is ever rendered entirely unnecessary, we shall be close to rendering people unnecessary.

People are the essence of the office. Conforming – usually willingly – to certain norms of dress and manners, they are on their best behaviour in the office (see them at home) but nevertheless all their characteristics are on display. They probably spend more time with their colleagues than with their families, which means that for many the office is not just one area of life among others but the axis around which life revolves.

This book is for all, from cleaner to chief executive. It deals with handkerchiefs, humour, hope and heart-throbs. Sometimes it contradicts itself, like the office life it describes, but if you would test its truth, look about you.

Smile.

 In meetings, speak softly and carry a big pen.

 Dress as well as you can afford.

 Keep your desk tidy. Most very successful people have clear desks.

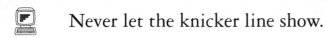 Never let the knicker line show.

Never be afraid to change a decision.

Praise whenever you can; showing you know the facts is usually blame enough.

Be considerate of bosses; they need help.

When meeting colleagues outside work, make a point of discussing something different.

 Never attempt to hide a tampon up your sleeve; always take a bag or purse to the loo.

Beware: information technology always does less than they said it would, takes longer, costs more and soon needs replacing.

 Beware again: information technology also does more than you need.

Learn the names of your colleagues' children; spouses' names don't matter.

 Keep two spare pairs of tights in your desk drawer.

 Don't swear; it shows lack of control and people respect you less.

Get an office as close as possible to the centre of power.

 If your phone rings when someone is talking to you, either ignore it or ask the caller if you can ring back.

 Keep your fringe well trimmed.

Wear waterproof mascara.

 Appreciate that office life is essentially the negotiation of power relations between people.

 Do not display personal photos.

 Avoid skirts with wrap-over fronts.

Don't kid yourself that an untidy desk means you have a lot to do. It just means that you're not doing it.

 Remember that PMT does not exist for female executives.

 Never neglect first impressions, they're often the only ones you have a chance to make.

When hiring, be clear and honest.

 Have the confidence to delegate.

 Never be without a clean handkerchief but never decline the offer of one from a male colleague.

Don't fight your colleagues, help them; some may be your future bosses, others your staff.

 Have faith in your first impressions of people; they're nearly always right. Don't trust your first impressions of problems or places, however; they can often be wrong.

If complimented upon your appearance, reply with a polite 'thank you' and no more, no matter what the motive.

 Don't comment to one woman on another's appearance.

When people come to see you, always put down your pen or turn away from your screen to greet them.

 Stay calm and never row. Let the other party row; they'll lose.

Retail harmful gossip only if it's advantageous to you, but not if it's obviously so.

 Never wear shoes with heels that clatter.

 For a long lunch, leave early rather than return late.

When firing, be fair, fast and firm.

 Don't be punctual; be early.

 Polish your shoes.

 Watch for the little things: they give people away more than the big issues.

Always make friends of caretakers, porters, cleaners and anyone connected with building maintenance.

 Look directly at people, if not in their eyes then at their lips. To them it usually looks the same.

Meet anger with calm, resolution and knowledge of the facts.

 Perfect your table manners. How you hold your knife and fork matters not because others may disapprove but because it indicates whether you are one of them or not.

If you want to win over others, ensure that you first possess yourself.

 Never wear a tie when your shirt collar is undone. Be either open-necked or properly formal.

 Either shave properly or grow a full beard or moustache overnight.

Be casual but never scruffy.

 If you must roll up your shirt sleeves, roll them above the elbow neatly and evenly, about four fingers' width.

 Don't despise conformity: it is a free state that permits great differences beneath the surface.

Buy good, conventional suits that are not subject to fashion, even if you're in advertising.

 If you're bald, don't try to hide it. Just don't think about it.

 Remember that office romances are easy in the starting and hard in the parting.

If you are late, make an immediate and formal apology. It may obviate the need for an explanation.

 If you want something done quickly, ask a busy person.

 Don't attempt conversation in lifts. A smile will do.

Don't laugh loudly in corridors.

 Bad backs are not helped by bad posture. Use a typist's chair.

 Either share your milk, coffee, tea and biscuits, or willingly contribute to the cost of common supplies.

Beware of managers who talk unceasingly about Management. They are invariably the worst managers.

 Remember: those who can, manage; those who can't, Manage.

 Be polite.

Appreciate your company car if you have one.
A company car – any company car –
is the best sort there is.

 If you are worried about your future, clean
your bike now but keep smiling.

Bear in mind that bosses like people who are resolute, bold and cheerful and who on occasion stab.

 Remember that there's more to work and to life than working to live or living to work.

Understand that getting on is largely a question of doing your job well and rubbing along with people.

 In any negotiation seek to occupy the middle ground; then you can dictate the terms.

 Don't hog the floor in meetings, but make what you do say count.

Don't worry about top salaries; watch the bottom line.

 When writing, aim to be both comprehensive and concise, and seek a style that is colloquial and precise.

 Mind your manners. Manners make the difference.

Don't forget that the three priorities in choosing your office are location, location and location.

 Know the higher laws of office furnishings: wood is good, leather impresses, a view delights and a personal loo is the ultimate.

Flatter. You can't overdo flattery; everyone believes some of it.

 If you think you are doing your job as well as you can, think again. People nearly always know how to do their jobs better but they don't always know that they know it.

Don't rock the boat until you know where you want it to go.

 Try not to be bothered by *enfants terribles*. They're really not so terrible; they simply haven't stopped being *enfants*.

 Don't be surprised when the office punishes you for being away.

Remember that office rivals, like rivals in love, should never be openly acknowledged.

 Don't manoeuvre. Identify what's right and go for it.

 Don't complain of stress while it helps you to cope better. It's when you're not coping that it hurts.

Remember the four ages of the wage slave: work and fun in the 20s, work and fulfilment in the 30s, work and pension worries in the 40s, work and retrospection in the 50s. After that you're a pet.

 Shed no tears for the 'stressed' top executive. Stress afflicts those who don't make it far more than those who do.

Treat office politics as a game in which the real losers are those who can't laugh about it.

 By all means consider yourself unique, but remember that no one is essential and no one irreplaceable.

 Aim to be both efficient and effective, and remember that they are not the same.

Mock neither God nor the Board, and remember that the Board is more easily offended.

 Learn Budd's law: a temporary measure will last the period first stated multiplied by the number of people who took the decision.

When making cuts, start at the top.

 Use short words.

 If the office gets you down, regard it as a game for the not yet grown up, and don't take it home.

Understand that the office functions as a collection of individuals, as a group and as an institution, tempered by the law and by the limits of goodwill and self-interest.

 Look for the most common characteristics among your colleagues, and you'll usually find that helpfulness is one of them.

If you want to earn someone's good will, ask an easy favour.

 Mostly lunch wisely but sometimes lunch well.

 If you have to do business over breakfast, get there first.

Don't write graffiti in the lift.

 Do business before lunch.

 When people lose their temper with you, either say nothing until they've wound down or leave the room. Don't argue, and let them make the next move.

When you're wearing a dark suit, always wear black shoes.

 Don't wear trouser suits unless you're stick-thin.

 When you want to look your best, wear a plain, well-ironed, white cotton shirt.

At office functions look at the person you are talking to rather than over his or her shoulder.

 Be ambitious, but not single-mindedly so. You'll probably get more or less what you want, but when you do either it might have changed or you might.

Don't waste time being envious and resentful of more successful colleagues. Envy and resentment corrupt, and gain strength by being shown.

 Don't criticize your boss in public, no matter how bad he or she is, but don't always discourage others from doing so.

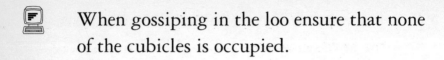

When gossiping in the loo ensure that none of the cubicles is occupied.

Be generous in praise, sparing in dispraise.

Take advantage of the privacy offered by the journey to and from work. Avoid colleagues.

Water the plants.

Never let it be said that downsizing is a term for brain shrinkage caused by the shock of rapid promotion to senior management.

 Ensure that you are not quoted as saying that delayering is a process whereby levels of support beneath top management are cut away without top management having to come down to earth.

When things go wrong, never blame top management: either circumstances (which it was not their job to anticipate) have changed, or the company (which it was not their job to control) has failed them.

 Don't blame the troops, blame the officers: there are no bad groups, only bad group leaders.

Don't try to look beneath the bottom line. There's nothing there but the edge of the page.

 Beware creative accounting: it means pretending the bills aren't coming.

 If you're having to write an appraisal, summarize it for yourself in a sentence.

Remember that for many people doing something worthwhile is more important than more pay.

 To make your organization successful, ensure that it believes in itself, establishes a tradition of achievement and is served by people who expect to be treated fairly but firmly.

Don't assume that fools are harmless. They usually do more damage than villains.

 Know the jargon but use it sparingly and never let it obscure the truth.

 Be careful with confidences. Everyone loves to pass one on, in confidence.

Regard any suggestion of an internal attitude survey as an indication that the organization is unsure of its purpose.

 Feed and foster morale. It is through morale that an organization achieves more than the sum of its parts.

 Keep people busy; they like it.

If you want to make your job more enjoyable, work harder.

 Don't congratulate yourself for earning Brownie points. They're OK only for Brownies.

 If you want to make changes you must give leadership and explanation.

Use bonuses to encourage good work; other forms of performance-related pay are usually expensive illusions.

 Don't use comparisons with other professions to push through changes for which there is inadequate internal justification.

 Never carry a comb where it may be seen.

Only wear a mini-skirt if you have good legs, and never when you want to be take seriously.

 Don't confuse the purpose of a meeting with its function.

 Imagine that you might be better than you think at making money, and apply yourself to it.

Don't call for nil returns. What's the point?

 Savour gossip. It is the wine of office life, the reward of all who tread grapes.

 Don't get into the habit of working long hours. When it's a habit it ceases to be a virtue.

Consider the possibility that your habitual long hours are a sign that you need the office more than it needs you.

 If you feel tired at your desk, get up and go for a walk.

 If you feel unwell, go home.

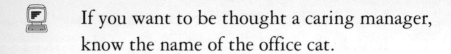 If you want to be thought a caring manager, know the name of the office cat.

Use clichés carefully. They are often true but they blind you to what is before you.

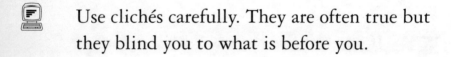 Appreciate that within each of your colleagues lies the potential for the entire range of human tragedy and comedy.

Don't kid yourself that the office is a microcosm of life; it *is* life.

 By all means bar pets and children from the office, but try barring fools.

 Be benignly bureaucratic and help things happen; it is bad bureaucracy that finds reasons for nothing happening.

Tell yourself there is more to life than the office, especially when it doesn't feel like it.

 Many people wear something casual on Fridays. If you want to be different, be smart.

 Remember that reputations, for good or ill, are easy to win and hard to lose.

Relax.

 Buy flowers sometimes.

 When dictating, include the punctuation.

 Say thank-you for good work. It takes only a moment but the effect lasts years.

For tea and coffee use Chinese mugs with lids; they keep it warm longer and are nice to play with in meetings.

 Don't be afraid to demand a lot from people. They're anxious to give, and most organizations fail either to demand enough or to show appreciation when they do.

Draw what conclusions you like from other people's doodles but don't waste time analysing your own.

 When your boss returns from being away, brief him or her thoroughly, show what you've done and make sure you leave something to be done.

If you're thinking of floating the company just to raise capital, think hard and think again.

 Don't squabble about the milk: meanness shows itself in trifles.

Be mean only when it really counts. Meanness in big things is called common sense.

 When you return from being away, ask your boss for a briefing.

Never admit that a task is too difficult; just show that it's inappropriate that you should be asked.

 If you're overwhelmed by a sense of unreality and confusion, don't assume you're coming down with flu. You may simply have been to too many meetings.

Do not to the increase of net profit admit impediments.

 Don't congratulate yourself too much if you have an idea. Having them is easy; implementing them is much trickier.

 Don't shoot the messenger.

If you wish to administer bureaucratic poison, get your enemy to chair the committee that allocates office space and rooms. No one is ever satisfied and everyone will blame him or her.

 Do not argue against an initiative solely because it might set a precedent. They probably said the same about the wheel.

Appreciate that meetings spread responsibility, which is not always a bad thing.

 If the best you can say about someone is that he or she works well under supervision, admit to yourself that it's not working.

 Never be afraid to dream.

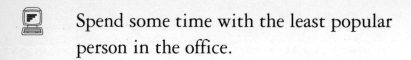 Spend some time with the least popular person in the office.

Don't worry about wasting time in the office; worry about wasting your life.

If you have to address any audience, stand up, speak up and shut up.

If you have to address a large audience, aim your remarks at the back wall.

 Don't overrate the importance of experience and don't underrate enthusiasm.

 For every right you claim at work, acknowledge a duty.

If there is no one at work you admire, move.

 Be efficient, but above all be loyal.

 Treasure the offices where you can still take your dog to work.

 If you can walk to work, count yourself lucky.

Use Monday for problems, Tuesday for ideas, Wednesday for achievements and Thursday for praise. Save Friday for crises.

 Before urging that we clean our own offices, consider who would empty the Hoover bag.

 Be first to say you are wrong.

Bear in mind that most people work better in the mornings. But know who the exceptions are.

 If you're urging the paperless office, understand that it is just a floppy disc away from the peopleless office.

If you're tempted to set up on your own, do realize that working for yourself is a 24-hour day, life-long test of character.

 Admit that everyone makes mistakes and remember that sometimes mistakes make people.

Don't allow yourself to think that the office is against you. It is neutral like the sea. What matters is how you sail it.

 When the office rings you at home, try to sound neither resentful nor relieved.

 Go home. Have anyone's last words been, 'I wish I'd spent more time in the office'?

Wonder aloud why all offices unconsciously discriminate against red-haired men, but not against red-haired women, and try to establish whether it applies to all areas of life.

 Boost office morale. Organize a regular whip-round for lottery tickets.

 Don't sniffle.

Be honest; you probably could get through your work in fewer hours, provided you were paid the same to do it.

 If you ever get the chance of a sabbatical, unpaid leave or a career break, take it.

Don't resign before finding another job. It's always easier to find one when you've got one.

 Don't resign in an emotional spasm. Do it in a way that's to your advantage.

Praise your successor; it is not in your interest that what you have started well should be seen to go bad.

 In times of triumph or despair, remind yourself that no news in the office is ever as good or as bad as it is first presented.

Don't assume that information technology always means fewer jobs; it may simply mean a change in job titles.

 Don't worry if you're support staff; you'll always be essential. How else can your boss feel like a boss?

You may well have seen it all before but try not to say so more than once a week.

 Try not to put all your trust in one set of figures, especially when they're all you've got.

 Don't neglect to audit the auditors, nor to account for the accountants.

Make allowances for commuters.

 Don't discourage a degree of sexual tension; it helps the office perform better. But beware sexual licence; it weakens corporate endeavour.

 Wear good shoes and good gloves.

Don't criticize your predecessor; let others do it.

 Keep an umbrella in the office.

 Don't read only the paper on the way to work. Try something more demanding and you'll find it more refreshing.

Imagine for a few minutes that everyone else feels as you feel.

 Try to make a contribution, so that you don't leave a job exactly as you found it.

 Most things may never happen but this one will; so get life insurance.

Send not to know for whom the retirement party calls; it calls for thee.

 Avoid bright pink lipstick.

 Don't be overimpressed by people who use smart pens.

 Keep smiling.

Don't boast of killing time; it's the other way round.

 If you return to work to find you've forgotten everything about your job, be encouraged. It's the sign of a good holiday.

 Don't be afraid to bring a meeting to a close. No one will blame you for it.

Don't eat crisps in the office. Try an apple.

 Get your pension sorted out.

 Try to notice only good things about people you work with, because once you've noticed anything bad about them you can't forget it.

Try not to make enemies, but if you do, try to forget them.

 Don't always eat in the staff canteen and don't always avoid it.

 Be attentive. Attentiveness is flattering.

Accept that favouritism is as inevitable as it is wrong and that the choices are sometimes right.

 Show some sympathy for the personnel department. They get few thanks and nearly all the problems.

If you win promotion, try not to regard it only as belated recognition of your obvious merit. If you are rejected, don't assume that it's simply a fault in the system.

 Learn from the competition but don't worry about it.

Be cheerful, helpful and good at your job. You'll find there really isn't any competition.

 Don't worry too much what your colleagues think of you. For the greater part of their lives they aren't thinking of you at all.

There are many more would-be plotters than actual plots, so don't think that every ill-wisher is part of a conspiracy.

 Make sure you realize that the good times at work are good; it makes them even better.

If you're having a bad time at work tell yourself that that's all it is; work is not the world and the bad times are not for ever.

 If character appears to be destiny in the office, remember that history is arbitrary.

 Acknowledge, at least in private, your failures. Recognition is half the battle.

Consider a stroke of luck to be chance, but regard consistent good or bad luck as an aspect of character.

 There is something beautiful to be seen every day. Look for it.

 Don't complain: the office is generally fairer than life.

Just because a task is hard, don't think that it must therefore be worthwhile.

 Try to create your own luck.

 Count the new initiatives and, as they mount, use your nose to detect the reek of self-interest.

Relish the satisfaction of a job well done, and being appreciated for it. There's nothing else like it.

 Forgive forgetfulness in your boss but not in yourself. In your boss it is a teasable, lovable little fault; in you it's a shortcoming that needs attention.

To cure forgetfulness, get in early and take an interest in what you're doing.

 Initials and acronyms are with us to stay, so don't be rude about the CEO's PA.

 Seek the devil in the detail. He's always there.

Beware the urge to be busy.

 Master the facts.

 Use detail to deflate bullies and bluffers.

 Don't think that the old ways are necessarily best, nor the new ways necessarily better.

If you want to appeal to a woman, start by listening to what she says.

 Before accepting any unsupported assertion, try the opposite; it's often equally true, or untrue.

Look at the faces in the office around you; that's what you are, or are becoming.

 If sharing a taxi makes you feel there's an intimacy already established, tell yourself there's no need to go further.

Think of the office's worst manager, and you'll probably find someone who is well qualified in management.

 Imagine that you know you are going to die on the way home, then think what you would do in the office this afternoon. Don't do it.

Pretend for a while that you are one of your own customers or clients, and see how it feels.

 Don't worry too much about getting what you write right; get it written and then get it right.

Think about it: money exists only if it moves and the faster it moves the more there is.

 Be considerate. Consideration is the essence of good service.

 Regular late workers should try leaving on time now and again. See if you can.

Never blame; it's usually a waste of breath.
Just concentrate on getting things right.

 Listen to advice. Good advice is often
expensive but the best is free.

 Ask yourself what you achieved today.
Answer to yourself, honestly and privately.

Plan for the day when all the computers fail.

 Don't use/deploy dashes/strokes when you could/might say it more clearly/simply and be honest/truthful about what you mean/intend.

If you're thinking of hiring consultants, try putting down in a sentence what they might say. Then think again.

 Try to give your junior staff the chance to do more than is generally asked of them.

Tread carefully. There are bound to be deep, hidden wells of resentment among some of your colleagues.

 Remember that among the same colleagues there may be untapped springs of devotion.

 Don't trust entirely to method and organization: personality matters.

Be selectively indiscreet: the pleasure of learning a secret is exceeded only by the pleasure of telling it.

 Don't be sentimental about organizations. Companies, like nations, have no friends, only interests.

 Choose tea and biscuits for flirtation.

You may marry your spouse and remain wedded to the office, but remember that the office is not wedded to you.

 To get an idea of how the office will manage without you, think of someone who left a while ago. Who thinks of them now?

Ask yourself whether you actually need a boss.

 Don't let promotion mean that you cease to do what you enjoy and do well, and so become one of the obstacles in the way of those still doing it.

Consider how the mighty are chosen: they choose each other.

 Look carefully at staff who are often ill. Are they happy in their work?

 If you have a job you can call a career, count yourself lucky.

Before you tell, count the many willing ears between these four walls.

 Don't overrate intelligence; motivation is more important.

 Don't talk over your juniors before they've finished their sentences. It's rude.

Never despise imagination: the value of money is sustained by a collective act of imagination.

 Pile on flattery with a JCB. The victim may reject most of it but will still feel that you're essentially right.

Most high achievers are workaholics: treat them well when you employ them because one day soon they'll employ you.

 Fight against the bureaucratic tendency to compartmentalize everything in life. Once you start it's hard to stop.

Don't be facetious in office notices.
It never works.

 When the office is dull, buy a bottle of
champagne. You need no better reason.

 Don't be surprised that so many lovely
gifted girls work for impossible men.

Look upon your career with pessimism of the intellect, optimism of the will.

 Accept that in most bureaucracies it is even harder to stop doing something than to start.

 Never describe an over-fussy man as an old woman: it's an insult to old women.

Don't expect to learn new lessons in business. There are none, only the old ones, again and again.

 Don't keep talking about how things used to be; newcomers think the past has nothing to do with them.

 Take your secretary to lunch.

If your boss asks you to lunch, always accept, don't try to go Dutch, and be very grateful. Bosses like to feel generous, once in a while.

 When there's a holiday atmosphere in the office, encourage it. Work will still get done.

 Think of the best qualities of the best boss you've had and try to emulate one of them.

By all means put the young in charge, but who will move them before they get old?

 Don't apologize for being grey and boring on the grounds that you work in an office; it's nothing to do with the office.

Don't worry about passing your prime;
by the time you think of it, you already have.
The secret is: it doesn't matter.

 Define maturity as the acceptance of
responsibility.

Approach office dalliance as an art, not a wrestling match.

 Whatever is happening, remind yourself that there really is worse trouble at sea.

 Don't just blame the Board. Become a shareholder and ask questions.

Make lists. There's much pleasure in ticking them off, or tearing them up.

 Remember to read your diary.

 Now – without looking at your diary – try to remember when your next meeting is and what it's about.

To have a real break, take leave for at least three weeks.

 Be thoughtful and determined and be lavish with care: that's what makes the difference between a good product and a bad one.

 Take joy in a thing done well.

Try today, just once and in one area, to do your job better.

 Remember that friendship corrupts.

 Do not allow All Fool's Day to pass unhonoured. An office that does must be poor in spirit and rich in fools.

Tell yourself that there really is life after the office, and don't forget that there really is life within it.

 Forget the future. That was, and this is, your real life.

 Talk to cleaners, guards, porters, messengers and maintenance staff. You'll learn.

Wash your own cup every day.

 And not only yours.

 Don't be blind to the present by thinking only ahead.

 Seek some reason to rejoice, here, now, this minute, in this office. There is one.

Judge a woman by her earrings,
a man by his shoes.

 When a colleague suffers bereavement,
neither avoid nor force the subject.
Look for ways to help and make it
easy to take time off.

Counsellor, counsel thyself, and at thine own expense.

 Buy some more flowers.

 Once in a while, wear something flamboyant to work.

Remember that involvements with married men are always either less or more involving than you want.

 Don't think of reaching the top unless you have health, stamina, determination and luck. Ability is not always required.

Expect things to go right even though they so often go wrong. They more often go right.

 Don't be too preoccupied to notice the birds, the trees, the flowers and the clouds.

 Better not.

Don't do the devil's work for him. He doesn't need it; he's a workaholic.

 Don't blame the Board; they were probably thinking about their pensions.

 Surprise yourself, if you can.

If you can't be wise before the event, at least don't remain unwise after it.

 Consider whether you would continue your job if you didn't have to work. If it takes more than a moment, you are already very lucky.

Don't set up on your own unless you have courage, plus everything else.

 Remember that the more senior you are the more important it is for you to show your face at office parties, and leave early.

Listen to people. They will listen to you more if you do.

 Understand that although gossip feels like a waste of time it often isn't, and that although work is not supposed to be it often is.

Treat gossip with journalists, PR people and personnel officers as work.

 Admit that you do your job more or less well and hope to get by, then reflect that it's the same with doctors.

Don't assume that any of the persuasive professions can afford to be completely honest. Clients, readers, viewers, voters and buyers neither expect nor accept it.

 If a thing is worth doing, do it.

Watch out for 'no doubt' and 'doubtless': they are most often used only when doubt is possible and the speaker or writer wishes it wasn't.

 Mistrust anyone who assures you that he or she is being honest with you.

Consider honestly what you have contributed today.

 Men – don't bemoan the fact that you have to wear a suit every day. Be grateful for the convenience; for a woman, dressing smartly requires much more thought and expense.

Women – don't begrudge the thought
and expense that goes into dressing
smartly: think how boring it would
be to wear the same suit every day.

 Don't clock-watch. Time passes more
quickly if you are busier.

Be positive. But remember that it sometimes takes more courage to be negative.

 If you're tempted by job adverts, write one for your own and see how it compares.

 Travel first class whenever you can. It's really not worth the money, so regard it as an affordable luxury.

Travel at company expense whenever you can, even though you hardly ever get time to enjoy it.

 Always have in mind another job you could do in the company in case you were asked tomorrow.

If you can't remember a name or a face, be frank about it and stop trying to pretend you can.

 Concentrate and take an interest; that way you'll remember names and faces and you might stop repeating yourself.

Think carefully about what you would miss most about your job, apart from money.

 Regard first wealth as health.

 Be cautious when making new rules and regulations. They may create more breaches than they prevent.

Try not to be the seventeenth person today to ask someone how their wedding or holiday or operation went. You can usually find other ways to show interest.

 Don't walk around in your stockinged feet, even in your own office. You will be taken less seriously.

If you're losing your hair, keep what little you have cut short.

 Don't be silly: there's no such thing as a tasteful tattoo.

 Pause before showing anger. There's nearly always a better way to put it.

When setting a deadline, allow for a secret reserve.

 Never be late with anything unless by agreement.

 Make sure that more laws don't mean less rule of law.

Don't worry: there's only one deadline that really counts and with luck that's still some way off.

 Bored? Fed up? Apathetic? Can't be bothered? Whose fault? Know thyself.

 Don't despise discussing the weather when you get to work; it's interesting.

Never commission murals for the office; they're usually bad and they date as rapidly as the career of the person who commissioned them.

 Let the habit of work be sustaining but don't let habits of thought and feeling deaden you.

 And now look in the mirror.

Think of the time when you will have no salary.

 Remind yourself that people are generally at their best in the office.

 Sometimes aim low, think small and count the pennies.

Think of the office as a comedy, even if the humour seems cruel.

 If you want to know who would work for your rival, look about you.

 To be happy in your work is a blessing. Don't take it for granted or think it your right.

Ensure that information technology in making you data rich doesn't make you information poor.

 Don't worry if you see yourself developing a parallel life on computer: luck, humour, obstinacy, irrationality, idleness and imagination will be with you always.

Ask yourself whether large companies can ever be purely entrepreneurial, or whether they spend too much time looking after themselves.

 Don't assume that because large organizations tend to be less efficient they are also less effective.

Be cash rich.

 Seek credit for achievement, but don't seek sympathy for long hours.

 Think of it as your money rather than the company's, and consider what you would have done differently today.

Remember that for those who work for themselves there is no such thing as time off.

 Look around you in the lunch queue, and you'll see the best and worst of human characteristics.

 Clean the mouthpiece of your telephone.

Call yourself complex if it pleases you, but we're all simpler than we think.

 Sneeze quietly.

 Don't be disappointed if the new job isn't quite as good as you hope; the old one wasn't quite as bad as you say.

Don't blame your computer for your own errors.

 Accept that you will have to make more effort with the social demands of professional acquaintance than with the deeper demands of friendship.

 Don't just moan, act.

Extend your learning curve if you like, but don't forget that eventually it becomes a circle.

 Pay the piper, call the tune, but don't try to play it yourself.

Be wary of statistics: because some Welsh
people are legless, or have only one leg, the
average number of legs per person in Wales
is 1.9 something; therefore most people in
Wales have a higher than average number
of legs.

Don't forget that we are all unique, average, different, alike and members of majorities and minorities.

 Before accusing your company of lacking talent, make sure you've given it purpose and organization.

Keep the twin horrors of office life constantly before you: they are, firstly, that it feels as if it's going on forever; secondly, thank you and goodbye.

 Call for them now, the powers that were, and await the echo.

Castrate Young Turks by promoting them.

 Ask yourself what, precisely, should be the function of a personnel department. If the answer is not obvious, consider whether you need one.

Accountants and people in Finance long to be treated as members of the human race. Treat them better than that.

 Seek achievable change and don't insist on the ideal.

Don't let other people have their cake and eat yours.

 Be imaginative. Bureaucratic imagination is as valuable as any other kind, and possibly rarer.

Resist the constant temptation to let the good drive out the best.

 Lift your product from bad to adequate by effort, from adequate to good by thought, from good to best by attending to detail.

Polish the boss and help him to shine, especially in company.

 Waning enthusiasm is natural. Don't blame the job; seek alternatives.

 If you've borrowed anything recently, check whether you still have it.

Always carry a clean handkerchief, and if you have to lend it to a female colleague, don't ask for it back.

 Try to exaggerate slightly less than everyone else.

 Make time rather than wait to find it.

Tell your staff that all work and no play sends Jack and Jill over the hill.

 And that all play and no work soon means just that: no work.

Don't argue for change simply by saying that those who oppose it are against change: think of something better.

 Watch rain through the office window. It's good for you, like resting your eyes on a green view.

If you want to resist change, do more than describe it as change for change's sake.

 Decide on the basis of argument, not assertion.

 Be warned: you have a duty to be logical because you have a duty to be honest.

Be wary of weasel words: they smuggle in unacknowledged judgements.

 If you must be dishonest, use long words because more can be hidden beneath them.

 Be clear about what you want to say and you will realize how to say it.

Think about which of your colleagues you would trust on a life raft. Don't worry; it may not come to that.

 Think about which of your colleagues you would like to go on holiday with. Be careful; it may come to that.

Learn to like commuting. It isn't all bad.

 Beware living above the shop because it usually means living for it and in it.

 If you want real money, make it, don't wait to earn it.

The meek shall inherit the earth and the poor in spirit the kingdom of heaven; think yourself lucky to get a terminal bonus.

 Divide people into eaters and eaten if you like but remember we're mostly scavengers.

Tap into all the talent about you, and yours will be the most successful outfit in the business.

 Cure all the backache about you, and you'll never need to work again.

The world doesn't always see us as we see ourselves. Don't resent it; try to understand the world's point of view.

 Watch out for resentment: it is the most common cause of disloyalty.

If you're a habitual hard worker, try coasting for the odd day to take stock and remind yourself why you're doing it.

 If you're habitually lazy, try working hard for the odd day. It might make you happier.

There is no end to self-justification and no limit to self-delusion, so don't think you're immune.

 Beware the danger of taking very attractive people either too seriously or not at all seriously.

Practise learning names, numbers and agendas by heart. It always impresses.

 Don't despair if your attempts at self-improvement don't seem to get anywhere; what is important is the attitude exemplified by the attempt.

Mistrust people who talk constantly of being 'tough'; they are more likely to worship the quality than possess it.

 Pick up a pen. You'll think better.

 If you would be tough-minded, be clear-sighted.

Don't rely on ability, charm and imagination to get you to the top. You should also be grey and pear-shaped.

 Look again at your pension arrangements.

 Ask yourself how often you think about anything at work for more than a minute.

Don't be disappointed if you don't make it to the Board. They always feel that the place for originality and brilliance is down in the company, producing the goods.

 Let the office teach you how to talk to people: learn to listen.

Be prepared for retirement to reveal to you the hidden truth that most people have jobs to avoid work.

 Check every morning that your chair, desk and screen are properly positioned and don't lift heavy files while sitting.

Don't swivel in a chair that doesn't have a swivel.

 Flirtation is the tomato ketchup of office life. Don't shake the bottle when the top is loose.

 Don't expect your spouse to believe that you need a flat in town for entertaining clients.

If you're ill, stay at home rather than infect your colleagues.

 Don't forget that we mostly are what we look.

 Don't be misled by unhelpful distinctions between work and play: it is purposeful activity that counts.

Never regard politeness as a waste of breath.

 If someone is rude on the telephone, be even more polite than usual; it puts you in control.

 When you travel for the office, bring back presents for those who don't.

Don't think that because you have power you have authority; only respect can bring you that.

 Be aware of a track running parallel with everything that happens, right alongside. It's called humour.

Ask before you order: people often perform with a better will.

 Recognize reality. That's what common sense is.

 Dress better; you'll feel better and work better.

Keep your nose clean.

 Pity the poor lawyers, if you can find one.

 Beware those who accuse others of ambition.

 Don't disdain stockings and suspenders;
they're legitimate weapons of office warfare.

Don't wear pens in an outside pocket.

 Think of commuting as a trade-off, not a compromise.

 Come on, smile.